CCSS Genre Realistic Fict

M000282154

Essential Question
What motivates you to accomplish a goal?

CHANGING GOALS

BY VIVIENNE JOSEPH • ILLUSTRATED BY CARLOS AON

"The tryouts for the competition team are tomorrow," Maggie told her older sister, Lori. "I need to improve my defensive play, so can you help me?"

"Sure I can!" Lori replied with a smile.

"Quick—you've got to be quick," Lori drilled her sister as they practiced together. "It's your job to stop your opponent from receiving the ball," Lori explained, and she showed Maggie how to use her body, arms, and hands as barriers.

"If your opponent gets the ball, then you've got to stop her from dribbling past you," said Lori, bouncing the ball to Maggie. "Now, try getting past me, and I'll show you just what I mean."

But no matter how hard Maggie tried to dribble around her, Lori was always there. Her older sister's long arms and legs seemed to have grown even longer somehow, and she blocked Maggie in every direction.

Lori could sense Maggie's increasing frustration. "Come on, little sis, don't get upset. Let's swap and see if you can keep me from getting through, instead."

That was nearly as bad: Maggie tried and tried, but Lori always managed to dribble the ball around her. Then, just as Maggie was about to give up, she finally blocked Lori.

"Yahoo! I got ya!" Maggie yelled in delight.

"Great work! You've really improved." Lori high-fived her and then added encouragingly, "Now go wow your coach."

Maggie grinned, because Lori didn't often praise her like that.

Vanessa was waiting for Maggie outside the school gym when she arrived. "Do you think we'll make the team?"

"Sure we will," Maggie said with a smile, still feeling confident after her practice session with Lori. Maggie had memorized her defensive moves the way a dancer practiced the steps of a dance—slide steps, back steps—and she knew that Ms. Gomez, the team's basketball coach, would be impressed. "We've certainly worked hard, so let's hope it's enough."

As usual, practice started with stretching exercises, followed by dribbling, some passing routines, and a free-throw relay.

Ms. Gomez then assigned the players to two teams, handing out two different colors of practice pinnies.

Ms. Gomez smiled and said, "Okay, everyone, get out on the court and in position. Go!"

"Good luck," Maggie whispered to Vanessa as they ran out onto the basketball court to join all the others on the blue team.

The game started with a rush, and Maggie prepared herself as one of the players on the green team, Jamila, dribbled the ball at top speed down the court toward her. Maggie went into action. Slide steps, back steps—the words came, and her body obeyed.

Maggie used her arms and legs like the blades of a windmill, just as Lori had taught her. Jamila faltered, and suddenly Maggie had possession of the ball. She faked a pass to Sharon and then turned and threw it to Amy instead, who charged up the court. This was followed by a quick pass to Rosa, who was standing unguarded beneath the basket—and the play was over. Rosa shot the ball straight into the net, and the blue team scored.

The players returned to their starting positions, and the game continued. Once again, Maggie managed to get possession of the ball, and she began to dribble down the court and around the opposing players.

Jamila started her defense, and Maggie glanced around, calling Vanessa for backup. But as Maggie turned, her foot slipped, and she crashed to the floor. She cried out in pain as her arm folded beneath her.

Ms. Gomez rushed over. "Where does it hurt?" she asked.

Maggie cradled her right arm and shuddered. "I think it's broken," she whispered tearfully.

Chapter 2

Thinking Outside the Box

Vanessa waited with Maggie in the nurse's office. "I can't believe it!" Vanessa kept saying. "I know you were a definite for the team. How unlucky can you get!"

Maggie closed her eyes tightly, trying to regain some feeling of self-control. She knew it wasn't just the pain from her arm that was making her eyes well up with tears. One look at her rapidly swelling wrist and it was obvious she wouldn't be playing on the team this season.

Her mother arrived at school and drove Maggie to the emergency room, where a doctor took an X-ray and confirmed that her arm was broken. "It's going to need a cast," he said, "and I'm afraid it will keep you from playing basketball for at least ten weeks."

Maggie returned to school the following day, feeling very sorry for herself. Vanessa approached her gloomy friend. "Come sit on the bench," she coaxed. "You can watch us play and give the team suggestions on how to improve."

Maggie studied the girls' techniques as they practiced shielding the ball, dribbling, and faking passes. Later she shared some of Lori's defensive tips with Vanessa.

As Maggie was leaving the gymnasium, she noticed the team uniforms spread out along one of the benches. She picked up a shirt, feeling sad that she wouldn't be wearing one of them.

Vanessa, Sharon, and Amy joined her. Amy held up a shirt, wriggling her finger through a hole and saying with a grin, "Not a good look."

Sharon nodded in agreement and said, "The team is going to look a little shabby, don't you think?"

"Yeah," Amy concurred, "especially once the boys finish their fund-raising and get their new uniforms next year."

FUND-RAISING
HeLP OUR Boys GET
NEW UNIFORMS

$500 -
$400 -
$300 -
$200 -
$100 -
$ 0 -

As Maggie walked home from school with Sharon and Amy, she said, "You know, I'm still really mad that I can't play with this wretched broken arm, but I did enjoy watching Vanessa and the rest of the team practicing today. I know I won't get to play in the competition, but I'd still like to help the team in some way."

Amy turned to her friend and exclaimed, "That's a great idea!"

"But what can I do with an arm in a fiberglass cast?"

Sharon looked thoughtful for a moment. "Maybe, since we're not on the team either, the three of us could do something together," she suggested.

Maggie nodded and said with fresh enthusiasm, "Now we just need to come up with a good idea."

That night while lying in bed, Maggie brainstormed ideas. She wrote "Helping the Team" in the middle of a page in her notebook and drew a circle around it. Then she wrote down each idea as it came to her. "Help out at practice; organize post-game pizza party; make and hang posters; design and distribute signs for people to hold up during the game." They were all good ideas, but none of them captured her imagination.

Maggie closed her notebook and turned off her reading light. Then, just as her eyelids were growing heavy, she had another idea. It was an absolutely awesome idea. She would find a way to get new uniforms for the team!

Chapter 3
The Cookie Sale

At lunchtime the next day, Maggie gathered her friends around her and announced, "I've got an idea about how we can help the team." Her friends looked at her expectantly while Maggie paused for dramatic effect. Then she said, "We could raise money to buy the team new uniforms."

"That would be great, because those shabby old uniforms are really awful," Sharon said. "But how will we raise the money?"

Maggie extracted her notebook and a pencil from her backpack. "Well, I thought we could sell cookies," she suggested. "We'll need some money to start with to buy the ingredients. Maybe we could all chip in ten dollars. Cookies always sell, so we'll get our money back, and I'm sure my mom would help us with a budget."

"I really like the idea, and I'm sure my dad will let us sell them outside the mall," Amy enthused. "After all, he is the manager, and they have community fund-raisers there all the time."

Sharon closed her eyes and said, smiling, "I love baking cookies—and eating them."

Maggie continued briskly, "I bet the school will lend us some folding tables, but we'll need someone with a vehicle to pick them up and return them."

"It'll be hard work," Sharon cautioned.

"Yeah, hard, but yummy and fun," said Amy, licking her lips.

After school, Maggie told her mom about her idea to sell cookies and raise money for the uniforms. "It's an ambitious plan, but of course I'll help in any way I can," her mom said, giving Maggie a hug.

She picked up Maggie's notebook and read through her list carefully. "I'm impressed," she said. "You've got most things figured out already."

In addition to organizing the cookie sale, Maggie and her friends began making paper signs to hand out at the game.

"It's so great you girls are helping like this!" Ms. Gomez said. "And we're providing a challenge for the boys' and girls' teams. The team that raises the most money before the big game will win new basketballs!"

"There's no way you'll beat our $500—not with cookies!" Jared and Kyle teased from the court where they were practicing layups with Jamila and some of the other girls.

Just then, Jamila dribbled right by them and made a perfect layup, the ball swishing down through the net.

"That's what we'll do to your total!" Amy shouted to the boys.

Maggie was extremely busy over the next few weeks, running here and there organizing the cookie sale while keeping up with her schoolwork.

When baking day came, Maggie's arm was still in a cast, but she managed to measure, mix, and bake cookies alongside her friends, and she only required help transferring the trays in and out of the oven.

"Don't you just love the smell of freshly baked cookies?" Sharon murmured dreamily. "I'm in cookie heaven."

Amy prodded her, saying, "Wake up; it's your turn to make the next batch of cookie dough."

Maggie looked around the kitchen with a feeling of satisfaction. She couldn't believe how many cookies they'd baked in just one Saturday afternoon. Everywhere she looked, there were cookies cooling on trays or nestling in the boxes that the girls had decorated and tied with ribbons. Maggie felt certain that they were well on the way toward reaching their goal.

That evening, Maggie and her mom checked everything to make sure they were prepared for the next day's cookie sale. Folding tables, money to make change, posters, tablecloths, napkins, a cash box, and lots and lots of cookies. Yes, it was all there and ready to go.

Maggie called Amy and Sharon before heading off to bed to confirm the meeting time and to go over their individual responsibilities one last time.

"We're going to raise enough money for the uniforms *and* win the fund-raising challenge," crowed Amy.

But after they'd hung up, Maggie's mind began to race. "What if something goes wrong tomorrow?" she thought as she tossed and turned in her bed, too worried to sleep. All kinds of frightening possibilities paraded through her mind.

"Bad weather keeps people from shopping at the mall, Sharon's dad forgets to pick up the tables, the cookies get crushed somehow ..."

Eventually Maggie drifted into a deep and dreamless slumber after counting cookies to send herself off to sleep.

Chapter 4

Results!

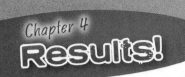

By nine o'clock the next morning, the three friends were outside the mall, with their posters up and the folding tables covered with tablecloths. All they needed now were the cookies. Sharon's mom had volunteered to bring them in her van, but where was she? Maggie looked anxiously at the mall clock tower.

As if on cue, her cell phone rang. "Sorry, but there's a small problem," her mom was saying. "The van just broke down. But I'm only a short distance away."

"Oh, no!" Maggie groaned. The worst thing that could happen had happened. "What about the cookies?"

"It's okay," her mom reassured her. "Amy's mom and I are reloading them into our cars, and we'll be there in ten minutes."

A few minutes later, two cars pulled up. Relieved, the three friends dashed over to help unload.

Soon the tables were groaning under the weight of boxes of cookies, and people began to gather around. Maggie had brought along broken cookies as samples, and the girls handed them out on plates.

"Mmm, homemade chocolate chip—my favorite," one friendly woman said, and she bought seven boxes.

Sharon rubbed her hands together with unsuppressed glee. "At this rate, we're going to sell out before lunchtime!"

After Maggie had sold the very last box of cookies, she glanced up at the clock tower. The time was 11:06. They *had* sold out before lunchtime, just as Sharon had predicted.

Back at Maggie's, the girls counted out the money into piles on the kitchen table, added it all up, then subtracted the expenses.

"Yes!" Maggie, Amy, and Sharon whooped in chorus. The total was $520. They'd beaten the boys!

On Monday, the girls rushed to the school gym to find Ms. Gomez. The coach was delighted when she heard the good news. "I'm so proud of you girls. Thank you so much for all that you've done for the team!" she said.

"Now all we have to do is focus on winning the big game," Amy said.

"Coming to cheer us on?" Jamila asked, joining Maggie, Amy, and Sharon as they strolled down the corridor.

"Don't worry; we'll be there, holding up signs and cheering our heads off," Maggie promised her. "We wouldn't miss it for the world!"

As Jamila, Vanessa, and the other girls on the team jogged onto the court, they waved at their friends in the crowd.

The referee's whistle blew, the game began, and right away, Maggie could tell that the two teams were evenly matched. At first, Riverstone was in the lead, and then Westshore, until finally, with just seconds to go, the score was tied at 40–all.

Riverstone had possession of the ball, and their player began to dribble the ball through center court. Vanessa blocked her, but the tall girl managed to sidestep the defense. She stretched and sent an overhead pass to her teammate, who quickly scored a basket. 42–40! The clock was ticking down.

Now Vanessa had possession. She dribbled the ball past a Riverstone defender and then faked a pass to one of her own teammates before sending the ball to Rosa. Rosa lobbed an overhead pass to Jamila, who grabbed it with a one-handed catch, spun, and aimed an outside shot. The ball flew high and sweet into the hoop. 43–42!

Then the whistle blew, and the game was over. Maggie, Amy, and Sharon clung to each other, shrieking.

Ms. Gomez beckoned the three friends onto the court. "Three cheers for our wonderful support crew!"

Maggie was beaming with pride. She had been forced to change her goals, but she'd still achieved a perfect shot— even if it had been through fund-raising for the team rather than through a basketball hoop! She couldn't wait to see the team in their new uniforms next year, and maybe even wear one herself.

Respond to Reading

Summarize

Use important details from *Changing Goals* to summarize why Maggie was motivated to change her goal. Your graphic organizer may help you.

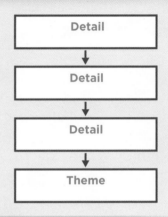

Text Evidence

1. How can you tell that *Changing Goals* is realistic fiction? Use details from the story to explain your answer. **GENRE**

2. How does Maggie's idea help her change her goal to one that she can achieve? How does this support the theme of the story? **THEME**

3. What does *tips* mean on page 6? What is another meaning for *tips*? What context clues helped you determine the meaning to use on page 6? **HOMOGRAPHS**

4. Write about how Maggie's experiences in Chapter 1, before her accident, help communicate the theme of the story. **WRITE ABOUT READING**

Compare Texts

Read a poem about students sharing their ideas about personal goals.

Today's Lesson

Our teacher asks us if we want to know a secret.
I wonder what this is about
and so does most of the class.
    We lean forward in our chairs.
Tyler stops yawning,
Kylie stops fiddling with her hair.
Mr. Jones turns to the whiteboard,
writes and writes.
Heads bob, faces strain to see, then
he stands back and points to the words
    A dream is a dream—unreal.
    A goal is a dream—made real.
Tyler yawns
(but I know he's listening),
Kylie loosens her ponytail
(but I know she's listening),
Andrew snickers.
Mr. Jones asks us what we think,
    what we think.

17

At first, no one raises a hand.

No one is prepared to take the stand.

Then finally, Benjamin does.

"Do you mean a goal like in sports?"

Mr. Jones says, "Well, you're on the right track.

Anyone else have a thought?"

He turns to me, and I am caught

off guard. I mumble,

"A goal is something you want?"

Mr. Jones smiles.

I blush.

"Benjamin? Is there anything you'd like

to achieve in your schoolwork, your life?"

Benjamin scratches his head. He's confused.

"Andrew?" Mr. Jones moves near him

and waits.

We wait for some silly reply.

Andrew looks thoughtful. "I'd like to, one day,

be president—if that's okay."

"Wow! That's a big goal. I'd call it long term.

Anyone else have a burning ambition?"

Silence again for a while

until, with a smile,

Mr. Jones tells us to "storm our brains!"

Brainstorm ideas for some goals.

We open our books.
Tyler's not yawning—he's writing.
Kylie's ponytail flicks—she's writing.
Our pencils fly as we write.
Our dreams soar as we write.
Mr. Jones says now we know our goal,
make a plan—
"Figure it out step by step, day by day.
Don't let your dream be beaten;
make it happen.
It'll take hard work, but it's worth it.
Remember, some wish their dreams
would happen,
others make them happen!"
Now we're all writing and smiling.
Our pencils fly as we write.
Our dreams happen as we write,
our goals.
And I plan my dream,
I detail my goal.
What it will take,
step by step,
for my mom's BEST EVER birthday cake!

Make Connections

How are dreams different from goals? Do you agree
with the teacher in *Today's Lesson*? **ESSENTIAL QUESTION**

How is the message about achieving goals in *Today's
Lesson* similar to the message in *Changing Goals*?
TEXT TO TEXT

Focus on
Literary Elements

Rhyme and Repetition Some people think that all poems have to rhyme and that rhymes come at the ends of lines. In fact, a lot of poetry does not have this kind of rhyme. Free verse poems don't use a fixed rhyming pattern, but poets often use internal rhymes to give rhythm to the poem.

Repetition also gives rhythm to a poem. It forces the reader to slow down or notice an important idea.

Read and Find The poet uses repetition on page 19, "Our pencils fly as we write/Our dreams soar as we write."

The poet also uses rhyme on page 18, "At first, no one raises a hand. No one is prepared to take the stand."

Look for more examples of repetition and rhyme.

Your Turn

Have fun with rhyme and repetition by writing a short poem using no more than 60 words. Try to make at least two words rhyme, and repeat at least one word or phrase. Your poem also needs to make sense and convey an idea, a description, or a feeling.

Then write several poems and choose your faviorite ones to illustrate. Make a collection of your poems.